Disrupting the Flow

Poems by Janet Banks

Kansas City   Spartan Press   Missouri

Spartan Press
Kansas City, Missouri
spartanpresskc.com

Copyright © Janet Banks, 2019
Second Edition
ISBN: 978-1-950380-22-0
LCCN: 2019938173

Design, edits and layout: Jeanette Powers, Jason Ryberg
Cover and interior photos: Janet Banks
All rights reserved. No part of this publication may be
reproduced or transmitted in any form or by any means,
electronic or mechanical, including photocopying,
recording or by info retrieval system, without prior
written permission from the autho

This book was orginally part of the Spartan Press POP Poetry
series, which ran from 2015 to 2018.

Some of these poems have appeared before
in *Stewed Soul* and *The Edge of Urban.*

Table of Contents

Global Obsession / 1

Straddling / 3

Haughty Winter / 4

Girl's Room / 5

Perceptions / 7

Victoria's *Shh!* / 8

Nocturnal Playground / 9

Black Ground / 10

Summer's Last Soiree / 11

The Purist / 13

Bare Intelligence / 14

Eden's Curse / 15

Gracefully Aging / 16

Lunch-Break Tango / 18

A Poet Romancing / 20

Armchair Voyeur / 21

Secret Sex / 22

Fool's Picnic / 24

Side Dish / 25

A Venus and Serena Rising / 26

The Search / 28

At Climax / 30

Acid in Your Tea, Party / 31

Bum Magnet / 33

Lady Bee / 35

Bitter Biddies / 37

Hormone Havoc / 38

M. J.'s Aquittal / 39

Iraq and the Pain in My Brain / 40

Politic Trick / 42

Twistin' It / 43

Post-Mortem / 44

Disconnected / 45

Hot to Death and Still Kickin' / 47

The Glutton / 48

Inside Job / 50

This book is dedicated to my Husband,
Stanley E. Banks, who is the love of my life,
my teacher, my ride or die, my best friend.

Global Obsession

Black, white, tan and red women
marching like soldiers going to war on a quest
to conquer and strengthen our self-esteems.
we all have a common bond of hair salons
full of fast talking gossip and
flying curlers in hair burning sessions.

Nail salons jump with the smell of acetone,
colorful nail splashes of gold, copper,
pink, coral, pewter and fire engine red,
clothing stores with tight-fitting rooms,
two-way mirrors, tugging, zipping, and laughing,
boutiques filled with accessories such as
big shiny gold hoops, dainty little pearls,
diamonds, belts and utility purses.

We are on a crusade
to re-invent ourselves,

keep it fresh and
play dress up like we did
when we were little girls.
Then we grow up in
our global obsession
where there are no differences —
it's a girl thing.

Straddling

In between youthfulness,
becoming elderly and watching
etchings on her skin change direction,
the first spot of red ladies,
budding breasts and puberty had
a fast hot-tail girl dancing with
her hormones trying to keep up,
walking with a blindfold into shameful
situations with madmen trying to suck
all of the good air out of her lungs with
mood swings and suicidal thoughts,
hell of an ordeal.
Straddling womanhood can be a
neat trick, and in between stages
like a dress rehearsal changing for parts,
clashing together like cymbals out of tune,
no balance, no synergy, just disarray,
one of these days the elderly wise
woman will take her rightful place
turning out-of-sorts noise into
a raucous symphony.

Haughty Winter

Winter begins her day
with an icy attitude,
high and mighty
causing all to bundle up
from her artic frenzy.

Summer tries to intrude on Winter's thrust
while she does her business of blowing
things off, being cool, haughty, naughty, breezy,
playing hide-and-go-get-it with the sun and clouds
daring anyone to come out
in the trap she's set for her prey.

She's a numbing mind blower
throwing shots of cold bullets
making Summer run off
with a white flag of surrender.

With her hands on her glacial hips
working her indifferent neck,
Winter makes her brash entrance
and is proud of her handy work,
so we better pack our lunch
because she'll be here for a while,
and we can't touch her
or we'll get frost bitten.

Girl's Room

Dropping a load
of male crap,
girl talking,
Damn, you got a quarter?
Aunt Flow just
came for a visit.
Applying and
re-applying lipstick
while primping
in the mirror,
Girl, that man …
I'm kicking his
ass to the curb.

Perceptions

Prisms from a light source blocking eye sight,
shadows of people moving in and out
of the sun, a vision of beauty from
a distance becomes an ugly mess up close,
can't figure out what it is —
a Picasso knock-off, a stew of vomit,
spots of color from scorched corneas,
black and white figures outlined on paper
ready to be cut out and balled up,
starting over on gingerbread dough flattened
out by a steamroller disguised as a rolling pin,
erecting walls of a sugary and spicy house,
children nibble and get eaten
by witches — which witch,
the wicked or the good one?
Seeing is believing;
is believing seeing?

Victoria's *Shh!*

Tits and ass hanging out
sashaying in front of God
and the world. Like it's normal to
flit around half peeled.
A high class racket to look demure
But teetering around like newborn *Ho's.*
Blue and red lace, sheer black push up
bras, panties and thongs
caught up in the cradle of their
butts smiling with pasty white
teeth and alabaster wings on the
catwalk with stilettos and diabolic pink
toe nails dancing with open legs
while the rock music plays on for them
to later graduate to a stripper pole.

Nocturnal Playground

The mind is a playground
for whatever one wants.
The night bird comes out
when the sun goes down,
and the moon dances out
bringing sleepiness to some and
in others an awakening.
Lovers come out of their hideaways.
Weirdoes slither out of their crevices
to be freaky all night.
Inside the sleepers are in their beds,
minds faraway while some of them
twist and contort in a
nightmarish chaotic cloud;
the mind at night is a nocturnal playground,
a host where anyone and anything can find
a place to play.

Black Ground

An onyx, ebony surface of shiny,

Sheer, opaque and soft like butter.

A smooth dark charcoal shaded black drop.

Midnight with no bright stars, just jet black skies

sporting an ominous personality.

A smoky, sable complexion or an ink blot

on white paper like a Rorschach test

popping in 3D. Blending, blending, blending

against the black ground of something that won't

absorb light, allowing it to stay supple and smooth

being wrinkle-free, not worn out, taken care of,

because black don't crack.

Summer's Last Soiree

At summer's end the heat is hiked up,
her last fete trying to
burn up everything
in eyeshot before she flits on.
Her heat was so disarming that
we could see Satan himself fanning.
The party's over.
Picnic days are gone.
She's played out,
and it's time for her to quit.
Summer started out so gracious—
thought maybe she'd be understanding;
that wasn't happening.
Everyone and everything
was weakened by her biting temper.
She did not respect
the beauty of the season
flaunting before her.

By the afternoon,
she had made her entrance again.

Being indignant was her
way of having an advantage.
Soon she must move on
and let Autumn check in.

The Purist

(For Stan My Man)

No diluting, tainting or watering down.
He likes the real thing, not a facsimile.
An instrument has to have its own sound;
every word has to pack a punch.
Contemporary jazz is an oxymoron.
He believes an actor must
inhabit a life worthy or not.
He likes the Count as in Basie,
the Duke as in Ellington,
the coolness as in Miles.
This *bona fide* man
is purely my soft spot.

Bare Intelligence

Cellophane brain, cerebral secreting
frontal lobe throbbing, e=MC2 equation
from Einstein.
A thinker like Freud, Nietzsche and
other philosophers from way back,
although Aristotle, Plato, and Socrates
had that think thing covered.
Migraine, head scratching in the
membrane, a proboscis of a unique
size has to carry a Brainiac through
the minefield of borderline craziness.
The prodigies who can sit down and
pound out concertos or poets who can
write blind sonnets.
Bare intelligence is the sheer curtain
inside a moving cerebellum that
produces the juices of smart Dom.

Eden's Curse

Inspired by the art of
Jennifer Steinkamp's
work titled "Eye Catching 2002."

The tree convulsing in slow motion
as the wind takes hold of it
making the limbs look like baby anacondas.
In the shadow it resembles
the head of Medusa
morphing back into the tree
with the synchronicity
of pain as it swirls and curls
because it is dying from having
its fruit picked.
Darkness and light cast
an eerie vision as if
Adam's grotesque face were
trapped in the tree of knowledge —
Eden was cursed that day.

Gracefully Aging

Aging is one thing,
aging gracefully is doing it right.
Looking in the mirror with
a reflection peeping back,
small changes are petrifying if
the mind is not accepting.
Old pictures remind
how things used to be.
Tucked away in memory banks
are scenes of things gone wrong,
but reality comes when
smile lines and gray hairs
have a mind of their own
to tease and frustrate;
at the age of eighteen
spandex was a friend
but not anymore.

The days of thinking
a girdle would never be
in the vocabulary have past;
now it's an important
part of the ensemble.
So cherish the girdle;
it's a close friend helping
the new shaped-up ass.
Age is not just a number,
it's a state of mind.
Be proud to look in the mirror
and say, *Girl, you
look just fine!*

Lunch-Break Tango

The smell of fried onions
permeates the air at
a local fish market with

hot tom cats slinking around
to taste the catch of the day.
The aroma is so powerful
igniting spicy juices to flow
into a cat's animalistic hunger,

causing a growling stomach.
It's time to feed the famished
feline. She hasn't eaten

all day. After her lunch,
lying in a pleasured state,
the pussy cat tilts her head
with slanted brown eyes
that look pleased.

She smacks and smiles with
greasy lips from leftover lobster
which seemed delicious.

When the clock strikes twelve,
it's the lunch-break
tango that stimulates
her senses again until noon
tomorrow, darling.

A Poet Romancing

On our fifth date
at his home for the first time
the television was playing
but we weren't watching.
The lights were dim,
it was steaming inside,
there was love in his home
that would eventually be mine.
Poetry seeped out of every crevice with
newspaper articles and art on the walls;
little figurines were inspiring and motivating.
Coffee cups from all-nighters stayed
on his table and desk; pens of distinction
with chewed up tops
illustrated his passion.
I knew this was the
romance of a poet,
a word doctor,
speaking in metaphors,
making love to me with
his intellect while pulling
me into artistic lust.

Armchair Voyeur

Peeping into the windows
of everyone else's lives
but never back in her own,
she doesn't know how to live.

She stands on the crutches of her
mother's skeletal memories
that keep her propped up when
living is too complicated.

She becomes a little girl
who tries to climb back into
her phantom mother's womb to hide
from her enemy called life.

Always in her armchair surfing channels
to watch other people's lives,
she's not in living color,
she's faded to black.

Secret Sex

obscure café with darkened corners,
couples sitting close together,
whispering in ears talking dirty
with feet under the table playing footsy,
it's steamier than the food on their plates.
The only thing needed to get in the
café is the nasty keyword
to the sleazy maître d' at
the door along with a twenty.
Couples look around to see if anyone they
know comes in when the bell on the door
rings a chiming song as it swings open and shut.
The café is full of couples of all
ages and races with hats pulled over
their eyes sporting sunglasses and wigs
that render them unrecognizable.
Many of the couples are feeding each
other in unison while others are kissing.

Secret sex causes condensation on
windows, and moaning sounds from
foreplay are bouncing off the walls.

After their meal, the couples either walk away
one-by-one or slink out of booths
to jump into taxis and go back
to hotel rooms or apartments
to ravage each other. After
their real hunger is satisfied,
they retreat back to their other lives.

.

Fool's Picnic

Pissed off, fooled, used up,
felt like leaping across
the fucking table
'cause I was falling on my face again —
I needed brains for lunch.
With my shoulders heavier
than a bag of canned goods,
I was livid about all the bullshit
my so-called girlfriends had shoveled at me.

Bent over, knocked down and
getting up after being danced on
like grapes for wine,
I told my fake-ass girlfriends
to bite me as I walked away,
licked my wounds,
belched out a so long sucker tune
and welcomed the ants
to my fool's picnic —
they seemed to be my only friends.

Side Dish

She doesn't want to be picked
over like cold French fries
with catsup, or lumpy mashed
potatoes with dried gravy,
over-cooked broccoli,
discolored carrots or slimy okra.
She wants to be the main course,
the hot and juicy meat like a pot roast,
prime ribs, or a T-bone steak thick and tender that
needs no condiments like A-1 or Heinz 57.
If she can't be the main thang, the one that
waters the mouth, tingles the taste buds when
swishing around on the tongue and feels good
going down, being the side dish won't fly
because when all is said and done she
can't keep remaining the side stuff because
it just gets pushed away and left out.

A Venus and Serena Rising

With much attitude on top
    in the rankings
they force their opponents into fear
strategizing quickly about
    when the next ball will fly.
their postures are fashioned with style
to smack the tennis ball
and make them stars.
      The teen queens from Compton,
       creations of a father who
      vowed to make them champions
       are fluid with their serves—
     possess power never seen
        as tennis ball whiz by
     110 miles per hour.
   The passion for the game
  was transferred to them
  from a mother full of easy fire.
   She taught them to stay
   strong in adverse times,

keep their heads up and
      tennis rackets ready.
        As young women with
      flowing braids and beads,
sequined and studded uniforms
          growing up in the public eye,
these teen queens from Compton
    are like twin Althea Gibsons
on steroids.

The Search

On a flight to structure
don't think it's for me
to be that robot in the blue / gray suits
with the shiny gold buttons,
opaque hose and patent leather shoes
to participate in that
daily dance of allegiance
to the corporate world.
I'm there for decades
like a child of Israel
wandering around lost
in a world so tight
unable to express myself,
an outcast in that society.
I do express myself
with a dark body tattoo
that won't come off
even if I tried.

My hair is my frame;
my face is my canvas
to paint my masterpiece,
my attitude of unpredictability
sometimes even I don't know
what to think about myself.
My plight is not in vain.
The artist in me will
never be structured because
I'm on a trip in search of me.

At Climax

Something clicked in me
when he strolled in.
My breath got caught inside my chest,
digging everything I saw.
Every arrow of Cupid
pointed out that he was the one,
and that day his soul made love to mine.
I didn't see him for two and a half years.
His image burned in my psyche,
his poetry massaged my ears,
his voice vibrated all through me
brought me to a delicious
climax of similes and rhymes.

Acid in Your Tea, Party

They are contortionists, their tongues
and their brains are not working in concert.
They twist and splay in all
different directions with lips
going from one side to the other
spewing out poison words that
incite hate in their acolytes.
Once they part their lips
They funk up the room
(and not the good funk),
With coco Mamie anecdotes
That stink like a backed up sewer.
They talk with confidence
about what the world should be
and look like and stand with the
KKK in secret. The dog whistles
massage the ears of undercover
racists pretending to be agents of
Our Lord and Savior Jesus Christ.

The religious zealots are all in
a lather from Republicans who are
so far to the right they have fallen
off … oops, they're gone. Their twisted
tongues are tied in knots
with foot-in-mouth disease, brains
still percolating from Satan's Sonnets
being read backwards to Hitler's
leftovers who have come back from
the dead. They are contortionists, their tongues
and their brains are not working
in concert, Umm, umm, umm.

Bum Magnet

The brothas who don't have their shit
together seem to gravitate to her.
Does she have the word *bum* carved into
her forehead with an arrow pointing downward,
saying *Here I am.* Raggedy-ass men
who are no earthly good with no jobs,
no homes and live with their mommas.
She succumbs to their weak-ass charm,
settles in because that is all she
thinks she's worth. Her mother
used to say, *Don't be with any*
man just to say you have one.
But she doesn't listen because she needs
a warm body against hers as she endures
hot funky breath with nappy, knotted
hair of men who think they're all that —
they sense her desperation.
The bums don't go anywhere fast
and suck up her time.

The clock is ticking, *tock, tick, tock, tick.*
Her mind is saying demagnetize and
get to steppin' but her body
still throbs for danger.

Lady Bee

While I sat in my car waiting for
my turn at the ATM with my windows
rolled down, the sky was grayish blue and
my windshield was misty clear.
The group *Urban Knights* were jamming
my song *Sweet Home Chicago* and the
music from the acoustics of
my stereo had the clouds bumping.
There she was a bright yellow and black
bee trying to enter my car.
I wanted to be alone and my fast reflexes
had my window going up with a
quickness. Lady bee moved to the front
windshield getting whipped back and forth
by the sound that was vibrating outside.
She was trying to dance to the music;
we moved and grooved together.
She fluttered and I bobbed my head and snapped
my fingers, and we were in simpatico.

The windshield wipers were beating her down
and she wasn't havin' it.
She continued to move outside my
windshield flying back to my driver's side
window. I heard tapping from her wings
flapping 230 beats per second while
we try to continue our dance.
The car in front was edging up slowly;
my new lady bee friend and I were
deep in a trance until the
song ended. She must have sensed
the music stopping and buzzed away.
I got my cash from the ATM,
pulled forward and hit replay.

Bitter Biddies

(For Male-challenged Females)

Belittled, befuddled , not at all bedazzled,
mad, mean, bent on beating up on male babes,
brooding, bubbling inside trying
to hide that real brazen attitude
being the brain of that operation
called a relationship,
a brawl at breakfast,
cause they think they're brilliant,
backstabbing, big mouth, bad, bad Honey brown,
lip-dragging, throat tickling, know-it-all because
she's a ball-busting barracuda, biding time
while waiting to bounce on blinded victims.

Hormone Havoc

Three females were on
each other's nerves;
one was a grown woman
with two daughters
and their attitudes,
up to her eyeballs
with the mouthy one,
waved off by the fast hot-tail
who could roll her eyes.
While they waited in
their own corners for
the flow of red relief
to come and subdue the
twisted hormones that
had them up in arms,
the men who couldn't
stand the red heat ran
until the chaos of
hormone havoc drained
and turned the three women
into purring pussy cats.

M. J.'s Aquittal

Deemed a pedophile
because he cared for young boys,
they scrunched together in every
corner of his huge bed.

The Pop star energized like
a skeleton moon-walking
out of the closet *Hee, Hee*
with fans adoring, screaming,
crying with bated breath
as M.J. waited on his fate.

The grifting accusers were
only out for his cash
hustling to fatten their pockets
while M.J.'s Peter Pan Persona
seemed to deteriorate, crumble
and float away to Neverland.

39

Iraq and the Pain in My Brain

A war is going on in my mind;
a war is going on in Iraq
trying to straighten things out
as things get foul,
attempting to slaughter the enemy.
The war in my mind is the memory
of my ex-lover's abuse
that won't let me rest
like our American soldiers
in Iraq trying to survive
by fighting and dying in a senseless war
like the ones I fight daily.
I can't sleep many nights like
they fear their enemy is about to pounce.
They're on their knees crawling through
dirt dodging gunfire and bombs.
Some get through the night, others don't.
I'm on my knees looking to God
for help from myself and
praying for peace to let me sleep.

Our soldiers pray to come home.
This irrational reactionary war has got to stop.
Those in power could have negotiated
before it got this far.
Who will negotiate for our soldiers?
War is supposed to be a last resort.
Why does my mind have to be
a constant battlefield
warring about nonsense?
When I pray for peace to ease the
nightmare of his brutality,
I need God to comfort my tired soul.
I'll pray for peace so our husbands, fathers,
brothers and sons can return safely back home.

Politic Trick
(For Sarah)

A sprinkling of smiles was all we saw
with square rimless eyeglasses, shapely legs,
and high-heel pumps prancing from one
corner of the country to another.
Political bamboozling, back-biting,
pandering, smirking with red lipstick on,
pimping out her family to the world and
perverting unknowing victims who straddle the
line turning them into rebels of stupidity,
everyone will always remember her
as a wolf shooting, looking at Putin on
a plane, can't speak a straight sentence,
President Obama bashing,
Tea Party hustler.

Twistin' It

Hula-hooping
and gyrating to
Martha and the Vandela's song,
Dancing In The Streets,
throbbing out of the radio.
We shook our little booties,
my sister and I
while my old Great-aunts
looked on with raised eyebrows
and curled up lips.
They scolded our mother,
Why do you let them dance like that?
My mother argued back,
If I don't let them dance here,
they'll be twistin' it
out there in the streets.

Post-Mortem

There she was, there she laid,
last rites, gone, disappeared from life,
her soul has left, she's done, the fork has
stuck the goose.

She slipped out of her old skin
and moved on, moved out, she has left
the building.

She quit, can't stand a quitter, the party's
over, she stepped off, respite, in stasis mode
sleeping peacefully.

What a nice person she was, because
death becomes her, her sun has set, last
show for all seasons.

she has shriveled like a raisin on a vine born
of a grape that use to house the juice of life.

oh, the sweet juice that used to make wine.
Now, all we can do is raise our glass and toast.